Unbind(ing)

Unbind(ing)

Asher Marron

Conviction 2 Change LLC
www.conviction2change.com

For my family at the Oakland LGBTQ Center and the Queer and Trans Open Mic.

Table of Contents

Rabbi Yoshua ben Levi came upon Elijah the prophet while he was standing at the entrance of Rabbi Simeron ben Yohai's cave…He asked Elijah, "When will the Messiah come?"
Elijah replied, "Go ask him yourself."
"Where is he?"
"Sitting at the gates of the city."
"How shall I know him?"
"He is sitting among the poor covered with wounds. The others unbind all their wounds at the same time and then bind them up again. But he unbinds one at a time and binds them up again, saying to himself, 'Perhaps I shall be needed: if so I must always be ready so as not to delay for a moment.'"
     – Babylonian Talmud, Sanhedrin 98a

"… her wounds came from the same source as her power"
     – Adrienne Rich

Preface

"You are altogether beautiful, my love; there is no flaw in you."
- Song 4:7

I loved women before I was tethered to time. When I did not know who I was, I knew I loved women. I marveled at their hands that carried the world; the stillness of their glance while holding cardboard signs, pleading and blessing;

the look that sighed, I know; their words that spoke of hurt and history. Their movements informed my own. Their language packed my throat with metaphor and offbeat rhythm.

Coming of age brings with it the knowledge of strength and survival. In my childhood, Catholic women,

whom I loved,

filled kitchens, parking lots, backyards, and pews near, but always a distance away from,

the altar. Their strength came in numbers, wombs that had birthed small saints, biceps that knew babies and bookshelves, and any other damn thing that needed to be carried. Survival relied on muscle, emotional resilience, and boundless devotion.

Every devotion is a devotion to women. Every sacred life came from the body of a woman. My Catholic women knew the sacredness of bodies. They prayed beneath windows depicting the Virgin Mary. Rivers of beads ran over their fingers while chanting,

Hail Mary, full of grace.

They wept with Mary Magdalene at the tomb every Holy Week. They reached for Joan of Arc's sword when subjected to the violence of being a woman in this world.

They were not writers. They were beauty. I knew I would be the writer of their beauty, their subtle aesthetics; their devotion to what is sacred, to what moves between lips and air, to flowers that venerate the earth when they bend but don't break.

These women compelled me to write about Mystery. In Mystery there is complication. There is contradiction. In Mystery many things exist at once. Growing into a queer identity is like that. I am bound by the circumstances that birthed me and free to realize my own purpose.

—

Once away from home, college introduced me to a cogent language of love, to express my love of women that had been ambiguous admiration in my youth, queer love.

My pursuit of liberating language liberated me.

At 18, I knew I was a lesbian; that my lesbian identity was sacred, but that this sacredness was not accepted in the Church of my childhood. Exploring my spiritual, emotional, and physical love of women in the midst of believing in the

God communicated to me by the Church was the opening and closing of exposed wounds.

The voices of men in the Catholic Church resided closest to my eardrum so that vitriol was never far. Growing up in a patriarchal Church taught me more about exclusion than love: you can be this but not that; if you are *that* you cannot receive the Eucharist; if you are *that* you cannot be ordained. But faced with the reality of being *that*, I searched for the voices from my past that spoke of hatred, sexism, homophobia and when I found them I realized they came from just a few sources. My conception of what was Catholic was formed by an authoritative few.

I had been ripped from the roots of Catholicism, the history of Christianity, the reality of Jesus' life; the sounds of authoritative voices of the marginalized muffled by fear of the power of compassion.

The internalized homophobia, internalized sexism, and rejection of myself was a somatic haunting of institutional discrimination; the resulting victimization of bad preaching. I would not make it through without taking up my own lance and pen to define myself for myself. I felt the doubt and curiosity of Longinus reaching into the wound beneath Christ's heart;

I needed to know for myself.

I am who I am. I am holy spirit and calloused skin. Freckled and female. I rebel against every morning and sing at midnight. Never well rested. I am brought to my knees at the sight of breasts and old books and Lazarus on the corner and memories of the woman who broke my heart. I shine whenever I say my name. I wince at the sound of women who say "like" every three words. I cannot forgive. Depression is my daily condition, so is resilience.

God marvels at me because I am an aching bridge.

I am a saint, sinner, and theologian of the capacious. I have been baptized and buried and resurrected by people and circumstances and words. I know that showing up is the most difficult and powerful spiritual practice. My tenderness is unsuppressed fury for the marginalized. I say *fuck that* more often the older I get. I've learned that mindfulness is a survival skill. I do not possess anything, everything passes away, and there is a boundlessness in the transience of this life.

This is who I am; this is what I know; and I struggle to understand it every day.

—

These poems are about how I found a way through. It is about the risk of radical self-love and radical hope for a reimagining of the relationship between Catholicism and queerness. This book came to life from the umbilicus-deep knowledge that I am altogether beautiful, that God finds no flaw in me, that nothing separates me from being fully human and fully divine.

I wrote this for you. I wrote it so you won't feel alone. I wrote it so you won't fear being both/and. You are marvelous. Truly. God beholds you and smiles. You, dear one, are beloved.

This book is my offering of restlessness, liberation, and love as queer as a $3 bill.

Movement I

Wanting

"Every woman I have ever loved has left her print upon me, where I loved some invaluable piece of myself apart from me - so different that I had to stretch and grow in order to recognize her…"
    – Audre Lorde

Offering

My paternal grandfather kneaded
dough blessed with thick hands;
I imagine them now
kneading with the devotion
of a Midwestern man.

My father has the same hands,
but gnarled from edges
of cardboard and sharp steel.
His herculean strength compliments
my mother's slim herbaceous hands.

Their parents carried them as children
loving with palms and knuckles.
Then they carried their parents
through age and illness.

Their hands are an offering only known
by coffee pots,
church parking lots,
doctors offices;
and now by their children.

Reflecting on this tender history,
I marvel at the ways we learn to be
historians of worlds we inherit.

1852
For Mills

Queer love laced the soil
where they built this school in 1852;
even the seeds knew
they loved women.
When my time came,
I found astounding women
who didn't take shit,
who didn't give a shit,
who gave no fucks about expectations.

This community reveled
in blessed transgressions hounded
for wholeness experimenting with love
and gender: our identities welcomed
like a homecoming in this queer place
that adopted us all.

The First Time

I believed
Mother Mary looked at me and knew.
Knew I was missing my God
wanting a return
to hear the sound of God's hair, laughing.

Every return to God
began with a woman who knew
something of me.
My very first was with Mary.

Mary listened
small words beat down
with the density of silk
while I was becoming something
to be seen, she could not look away.

Now an adult, I remember
what it felt like to be a believer.

4

I AM

God is burning
with His own name: I AM WHO I AM.

God is everything, everyone, no one,
every name, no name.
We bear a piece of that divinity that cannot be named;
you are who you are, you are plural, you are and,
you are all that came before and what will come.

God loves living in your skin
riding the air between your lips
the ways we are becoming
neonate and ever ancient.

Transparency

Transparency is a madness
that benefits only the one
seeking to be honest
and may never be met
with the same generosity from another.

What you want
must first manifest in yourself.
Even then the world may not meet you
but you may find that emanations of truth
are enough when they warm within you.

The Weight of Both

Attraction to strength
is a desire to be.
Self as a verb
a hunger to communicate
a famine of flesh needing
meat and weight.

Desire resided in the round of my arms
curve of my hips
iron in my calves
fuel in my feet.

Saturated through by gender expectations
I thought I could never have the density of men.

I became fully human
with a reimagining of my body
as a somatic text.
I wanted a coming out
without a coming out -
my joints and tendons to preach:

I am feminine

                                                and masculine.

Immersion

The women and men I admired
rested in my mouth
as ovate confessions
of beauty my obsession
possession in multitudes.

Dimples hammered concave
by the joys of resilience.
Licking my lips
swallowing atoms whole.

Jonas in the sea creature
covetous holding beauty
close for marveling.
I wanted to wear it;

I wanted immersion.

Permission to Look

I had to give myself
permission to look at a woman.
Cleansing myself of internalized homophobia
took years,

                            still

                                    lingers.

Admiration began as veneration
of the divinity of a woman's shape,
her moving through the world,
the places she hurt,
the way she looked
when no one could see her.

It began here:
giving myself permission.

Queer Roots

The roots of my lesbianism evade
language and accepted narratives.
It began with intimacy
with the world of women.
Intimacy is beholding
what a woman carries,
what she has seen, wants to see.
Sensing her gifts
welcoming her hardships in arms agape
to let her go with agapic love.

Every path I've pursued
aimed to serve women,
to be in the thick of their beauty.
My work is lonely, unattractive
labor giving language to their beauty.

My autobiography is the biography
of every woman I've met.

Like a neonate exploring
I keened and smirked.
Lesbian identity came like a prophet
and it became me.

Found

Language pulled itself around me
to make its bed.
My swollen iris
took in alabaster white
knowing the prophetic shadow of ink.

Language is limited and limiting,
it can talk around
but never get at.
What it does for me
is anoint, alphabets strung
in strands of curly hair to wash the feet
of those who expand limits.

Rugged

Patriarchy splintered me, to take
for fire the queer
drunk on ashes
from the cycle of dying
and rising beholding the real
God who wears my image.

Bicuspids broken
from chewing on God's form
and my animal wanting
of tree-shaped women.
Desire resided in my jaw
I reached out drooling led
language as dark as everything deep.

God swallowed clay
so I could be the rugged Word
to call all things by their names.

Skylab

The childhood my dad experienced no longer exists;
the physical and moral environment that raised him
dissipated in the '80s.
My dad knew records, rotary telephones,
the introduction of the microwave,
and an innocence that extended much longer
than mine ever did.

I am nostalgic for his childhood;
I wish I could have known it but I've come to
inhale it through family stories,
the kind of stories that get retold and never get old.

I roam through vicarious memories
of my dad's childhood,
allowing hands behind my eyes to rush over
wood and brick and tiny smiles.

Dad was connected.
His gang of boys reigned
over alleys and baseball fields.
They built the world of their childhood;
slapped together skateboards
just wide enough for one foot.
They tested their strength:
wrestling matches between my dad and his brother
resulting in lost teeth.
Everyone had a nickname,
that they still call each other as adults.

—

They approached construction in the alley
behind my grandparent's house
like the building of a kingdom.
Dad and his crew built a fort to rival all forts: Skylab.

Their plunder was salvaged wood, found nails, borrowed tools.
Skylab careened, it towered and yawned,
the refuge, the boys club: their own.

What was said in that place of their belonging
made God smile.

In the roof of Skylab they punched out
holes for the holy spirit;
a piece of the sky an essential element
to any visionary fortress.
The first attempt at Skylab taught them about building
something from nothing,
and the secret joys of privacy
for unregulated imagination.

It eventually fell but undiscouraged the crew rebuilt.
This time with a sturdiness and purpose of a fortress
to remain for centuries.

Skylab 2 endured.
A hideout for kids until that indescribable unidentifiable
time of being grown.
I don't know when it was taken down
or finally surrendered to the density of its divinity.

I do know that my dad smiles ear to ear
when he talks about that fort
built by his childhood friends;
he can still see it, and he remembers being young.

Photographs

Breath and instinct plumed from my solar plexus
before anyone imagined me.
Joy came before me, so did hurt.
Everything I would feel came before me.

God creates and recreates,
sonorous and brilliant humanity
revolves and returns to its origins.
Generations of my family calloused their feet
in fields snow treehouses,
burnt their tongues on Folgers
and microwaved potatoes,
and never ceased to kneel before a crucifix.

Divinity gets passed on.
I am certain every matriarch in my family was born with a
crown of daffodils,
a spine of threaded prayers and iron;
the spirit of ordinary saints meant to save a lucky few.

Photographs are precious.
They reveal a different time, the beauty of an age.
Black and white prints speak flesh and joy.
There is never a stillness in those photographs,
there is something animate about them,
which animates me.

Women can breathe in black and white,
they can be in their bodies;

without the distraction of light, I can see the quiet
boldness of their smile.

I can see them already savoring their youth,
preparing for a future of neon
and plastic that will never be their home.
Hands on hips or arched around a sister
became them, became their memories.

Knowing them as moms and grandmas was a privilege,
yet I've always felt removed from their history.
Their care for family directed their gaze
toward the future,
rarely looking back or speaking of what came before,

who they were when they were children.

The beauty that fills photo albums, an archive
for the recapitulation of family history,
drenches my mind in depths of caramel,
it is a warming of what preceded me.
That level of beauty feels to me unattainable
but I still seek it; it is my adoration.

Praxis

I have kissed at alphabets,
finding love through language
concealed in air and arson.
Language has packed my throat with smoke,
inhibiting and inchoate;
overwhelmed by the searing grief of being human.
Meaning has come to me carried in the air,
limning transparent space
like Braille for the inquisitive,
the wanting, the poets.

When I write, I am a drum
that thumps hard and resonates.

When I write, I shake my head at the lunacies
of being alive,
the lunacies of the systems that prevent
us from being fully human.

When I write, I am luscious litany that licks
at love and daily deaths,
the listing of who I miss with the ferocity of fists,
the gnashing of teeth and rending of cloth.

When I write, I am a hearse that transports
the dead back to ash and up into the trees;
a monarch that mollifies the pain of loss,
a reminder of transcendence, that beauty transforms;
a truing of death as resurrection.
When I write, I examine the etymology of women,

allowing flesh and lips and hands to tell their history,
what kind of language was professed before their birth,
what language they will confess
after they witness what passes away.

When I write, I am an altar to the Most High,
to the saints with the sagacious knowing of salvation,
to the women who speak fire
who snake their hips to poetry
of body positivity, whose bodies are art,
showcasing their hunger desire pull
of sex the fullness in their lungs.

I am a woman alone, gathering the earth around me,
the soil buries me it nourishes me;
prophetic teachings gift suffering
prismatic pain is my depth height width breadth.

Embryonic, dilated, womb-like, I am reborn
every time I write;
battalions besiege my vulnerability,
there is nowhere to hide.
Writing is the most intimate practice,
the praxis of living through language.

For You

I see you, dear.
You are not alone. *Do you hear me?* **You are not alone.**
Your attraction to the beauty of women
manifests in the beauty of your visage, your spirit;
I can see it.

> I know you and do not know.

Who you are is not new; you are completely new.
This tension will frustrate and liberate.
The object of your iris will careen and caress
at different times in your life and this is wholeness,
always grasped for always possessed.

The shoreline is a place to rest for a time,
but not for all time.
The river is flush and fleshed with gorgeous
remnants of gold from those buried and bursting.
You can never be buried beneath
although people will try,
but you will know that *you are a river.*

Revelation is in the body.
Who you are, and how you know
is a knock beneath the collarbone.
This is revelation: a rush of blood
to the tabernacle between your legs.
God communicates through the flesh

formed from divine breath,
God has a body and it is yours it is mine.
Desire comes from God; God became flesh
to be with us in body,
baptizing bodies in water
loving women men eunuchs saints sinners
martyrs prostitutes priests every holy spirit.

Every lovely queer soul is the body of Christ.
The ribs of Adam and Eve overlap
like a trans lyricism.

The art of sanity lies in the acceptance of fluidity.

Each of us born as a source of light,
a tiny collection of limbs and spirit
and wisdom bounded together in one boundless person.
We are an emanation of Mystery.

Falling in love with anything beyond the Self
feels like a remembering of the source and place
to which you belonged forever ago;
our voices an echo of lives already whispered
to us before we knew anything of time.

We are born seamless, already fluid,
possessing authenticity that generates wild laughter
until we learn of walls and words.

Oppressive language suppresses,
pinning people against walls;
the binary burns and mars.

The arbitrary labelling of what is acceptable
and what is not confuses
the beautiful and boundless.
For you, my beloved young lesbian,
don't spend too much time trying to make sense
of the arbitrary,
but define yourself for yourself,
broaden language so it welcomes everyone,
so language can be refuge not weapon,
a wellspring for the tireless insurgent.

Do you know that you are holy?
That divinity is in you?

Gender and sex are among the holy
mysteries of our rosary,
a knowing and unknowing, the object of veneration.

People may try to deny your coming into yourself
as a young queer person,
don't let them;
return to your God whose love knows no bounds,
return to your ancestors Audre, Gloria, Angela, and bell
who love you from the breadths of history.

If you want, I will tell the truth:
you will be rejected,
from something or someone you love.
As you grow and exercise your freedom
others will not know how to react,
they will be envious because they cannot be that free.
Know that you are free; no one can limit your freedom.

Rejection is a reality. So is love.
For every time I was excluded, I found a place that loved
me like Beyoncé.
I found places that celebrated my queerness,
where I could extend love to others for who they were.

Living as a queer Catholic is like sailing
a paper boat in a flood.
Survival is not expected, neither is ingenuity.
A storm threatens but the strength at the fold
keeps us afloat. We know the guidance of darkness, light
is not always necessary; we can detect
the yellow canary singing above,
and we know why she sings.

For you, young lesbian, I wish poetry
to pack your throat
and lavender to fill your eye sockets so you will
speak and see beauty
around and within you. I hope that you will discover God
in your own terms,
that you will know God as a living being of love
and the essence of queerness.

God is for you and with you.

So am I.

Footnotes to a Childhood

Writing about my childhood is a crisp spaciousness in my
skull/not everything lends to a cohesive story/
things remain, residue that wets my lips, demands my
attention/ yet is small, seemingly peripheral, but still
influences me.

---

1 My grandmother taught me to tie my shoes. She changed
my little life with laces and knots: she gave me a taste for
autonomy.

2 As a toddler my mom crushed my hand in the door of
our minivan and later dropped me out of a grocery cart. I
think this made me resilient.

3 Almost no one pronounced my name correctly growing up; I was unknown, misunderstood in a way that made me mysterious, a child of dense secrets only God knew.

4 I could never stand the comfort of night lights. Night is for the beauty of things that glow in my mind, and shaking hands with the monster under my bed.

5 Plumbing my heart for hurt and the heroism of childhood bursts open deep scars, allowing me to see how blood still runs and how to heal the pulsing pink parts of me.

6 Listening profited me; I know what I know because I listened to the words of iron and lilies, not the noise of smacking lips. Being quiet should not be cause of criticism for girls.

7 What is fragile and beautiful takes the place of what passes away. Every time.

8 I was once threatened with a gun because my best friend was gay. The boy who voiced vitriol and violence was never expelled, he sat at my table in Algebra.

9 I made my dad buy me a baby doll long after it was appropriate for me to have a doll, I just needed to tell my friends I had one, so I could be a girl.

10 Addiction and mental illness run in my family and that's all I'd like to say about that.

11 Not everything happens for a reason, please stop saying it does, instead tell me that you are sorry I hurt that I deserve to be free of pain that God cries with me; tell me I will survive and never really know why most things happen.

12 I am not what happens to me.

13 I am boundless and beloved and I will forget this when I become an adult; I will try to remember every morning over coffee and emails.

Movement II

Reclaiming

"God transcends all aspects of the spirit in gender and sexual expression. Such a God, who is all things in all ways in creation would not be bound by any human constructs of limits. Therefore, neither would Christ Jesus be limited in spirit as the intimate reflection of God in human form… Christ Jesus is the total human expression of the spirit of an infinite God."
– Megan More

Bone Dry

By divination or dice,
I was born bearing a family
chosen or given, I'm not sure.
Was I asked for
by a Creator wanting
to know me intimately,
to share in me?

Playing me like divination bones,
one thousand years old
enticing seances of the dead
threaded in my eyebrows.
Sagacious seers light my shoulder joint
on fire until bone could hold on to ink
for questions to be etched
on my soon to be sternum.

Will your throwing of ancient dice
bring answers from the other side
where the dark is luscious and wise?

Tell me now,
who rolled the bone dry dice
and saw me as the answer?
What was the question?

Indivisible

Names seep through
spew from salivating mouths
levitate from textbooks caress and create space
for rest within the openings of the alphabet;
I have rested my head in the crook of b,
curled up in u,
held my knees to my chest in o,
smiled wide sluicing over s.

Names are a respite,
an olive branch,
a fate, a guillotine.

We bear many names at once,
plurality is inescapable and joyous;
names can ring out sweet, others lance our side,
some remind us of our connection to everything else;
some self-identified,
others imposed to give others comfort
as they reach for words as we elude easy names.

Names domesticate what is wild within us,
they offer bastions of tidy phrases,
mild or outrageous, whatever someone makes of you.
There is an elasticity to names as they change
meaning,

either as we grow over time or lap up
nuanced definitions stated in the latest DSM.
How can you know your name
without gripping the lance to taste
the resilience in your blood?

Anatomy

Taken apart and unmade
by a culture that actively distances women
from their own genitalia
is a violence sustained through centuries,
reaching millennials by fiat;
fiat by men in power, religion, media,
the policing of health education
and reproductive rights.

Our orifices kept silent, shut:
a campaign to disembowel,
disconnect women from their bodies.

An immense dissonance keeps me
from my own body.
Embodiment is the power in my flesh
the agency permeating
between my thighs.

Genderqueer

"I have always wanted to be both man and woman, to incorporate the strongest and richest parts of my mother and father within and into me… I would like to enter a woman the way any man can, and to be entered - to leave and to be left - to be hot and hard and soft all at the same time in the cause of our loving… When I stand and play in the waters of my bath I love to feel the deep inside parts of me, sliding and folded and tender and deep. Other times I like to fantasize the core of it, my pearl, a protruding part of me, hard and sensitive and vulnerable in a different way…" - bell hooks

I am an embodiment
of the slender grace and ferocity
of my mother,
the solid shoulders
and kindness of my father.

All of it here in flesh:
cleft chin
freckles curves
stringent jawline
beneath round cheeks,
I possess.
I am all of it. At once.
Breathing gender up
and down my spine.

Vulvic tabernacle, I sacredly keep
for adoration, to touch its fragility.
I want to enter its vessel,
to be inside and outside
and lose myself in the symmetry.

In Praise of Darkness
For Kin Folkz

Darkness is pure wisdom
encompassing imploring
and so goddamn wide.

I search and find what is soft
pulsing tense vulnerable.
I find the God that has anxiety
over his hurting children,
who laps up water to moisten
his throat from so much prayer.

God is dark
dark skinned
deep womb, lush.

Without light God is everything, everyone.
God's transgendered features astound
demanding you behold them.

I am a magnanimous reflection of God's darkness.
The image of God I wear is succulent.
I am dark and expansive,
otherwise how could I be near God?

Movement III

Dying

"When Christ calls a man, he bids him come and die."
–   Dietrich Bonhoeffer

Genus

Catapulted from the embryo
I am a native of antiquity
or the mechanics of a satellite.

Youth never became me.
Always saying older
    and older things,
I knew wisdom to be
the letter z or the word
unrest or a name
on the spine of a book.

Not from around here:
a sonorous contemplative
seething in procedure,
teeming with why this?

Shooting myself up
    with beauty bleating
intravenous loneliness;
a woman drifting
amongst clueless crowds
    or do I just think too much of myself?

Once you could palm my mind,
squeeze it until the juices flowed
    you loved the taste
    and I loved you for loving it.

Now barren but birthing
clenching self-revelation;
my back arcs toward
the ceiling clutching sheets,
hinging on hips:
creature movements now habitual;
you've made me a
    genus of someplace else.

Geometry of Grief

One pinprick
and I am hewn.
Serrated in atmosphere
moving, just moving in space.
Body orbited
quietly overwhelmed
overt pain unnoticed
while the ordinary ensues.

Fledged at the intersection
flightless at the cross
striped yellow meringue.
Ten fingers counting down,
artfully measured movements
    hands in pockets
    soles strike concrete
    all at right angles:
geometries of grief in public.

Thrown hues
saturated light drench
my face draining
dimples of butter
fingers sculpt
until muscles are milk.

Spotlights dappled mercury
through honeycombed eyes:
    the letting in of toxic loss.
Sadness is photogenic

sensations syllabic
street sounds mask the threnody.

Neck thrashes,
snakes and twirls tense.
Jugular ballet
juggernaut of vulnerability
admitting defeat,
praising defeat.

Dower of daffodils:
my consolation prize
now thrown about
skirting every step;
unshapely regalia
    of loss and gain.

This is walking on the planet
collected disheveled
fucked happily alive.

Becoming Two

I am becoming two
people of the same rib
split down the medial line;
disparate modes of thought
stagger across
this line in the sand.

The alpha and omega
collide at the door
as I move from work to home:
silent combustions
like a chemistry
flask that boils
confident in expansiveness
purpose right down to the atom
then the fizzle and discard
and exit atmosphere
down through deep lunar sink.

I work then I do not
I smile then I do not
in the time it takes to walk
over the equator from my office
to other machinations.
My sullen strut
through matter
whether any of this matters or not.

My experience of myself
is narrator
of the two parts
two acts in a day

                                   neither is me exactly.

Every space has its rules
and practices its praxis
of boundaries binding
I tire of navigating.

I wish for expectations
of fluidity and authenticity
realness over niceties exchanged
in neon hallways.

I pull away
from shaking hands
and plunge my hand into the wound
of the valley,
where I am ready for the funeral
for the two of me
awaiting God to resurrect
one whole holy woman
from ash and poppy.

                                   I am Cain and Abel:
                                the resolved survivor
                                   and the perished
                             in exile for passion
                                    at home in death.

Requiem

Sprawled stasis
limbs forming passage
between flesh and sheets.
Emerald lines carrying red
from elbow to wrist:
sacred transubstantiation.

Talking up the wall -
a requiem for the ceiling.
Counting backwards
until the surrender
of masticated sleep.

A day of shape shifting
quarreled and quelled on the mattress
that will deliver me to morning
for routine postures:
the meditation of buttons and laces.

Counting

I used to count
the days of my dying.
Maybe tomorrow
there will be neon
stars peerless
paradise or Golgotha.

The way it was
rushing towards the rest,
packing our bags with light
leaving the past
sprinting to catch
a future of broken ribs
repaired by blessing
and a sagacious apple.

The way it is now:
a hell of remembering
like a haunting
dense and excessive.

Our boat built
in the meadow
languishes in floods
blooming gravestones
azure water ashen
running rapid with your tepid hair.

Your tongue planted in the garden
laps the molecular essence
of transplanted mourning.
Sowing or reaping;

                    who knows what is ordained.

Counting the days
as a wraith moving through
spacious grief.

Dark Prophet

It's a place
don't let anyone tell you different.
When you're really in it
    it's the epicenter of the ocean.

Swim or flounder
nearly drown
but traverse
    the distance stretch
across the width
lap up any nutrients
    along the way.

An island to yourself
no one else knows the landscape
not your pastor or psychiatrist.
Only you, dear.
It's your sacred ground.

The depths of loneliness
keen and swell.
Can you reach down far enough
    to touch the source?
Is it like electricity
    or a well in the desert?

Mental illness is a communication;
its own language
and few understand,

sometimes not even us.

It's temporary

it passes away
    but you know only for a time.
Dark is a part of you
    dark so goddamn resilient
    no one has any fucking clue
    of your strength.

By language or movement
or hook or by crook
distance and time
the fluoride of Depression
gives a gleam to your tarnish and doom.

You know healing is never done
there is always the cycle:
the mining and refining of salt.

Welcome suffering like a visiting prophet.

This is becoming human.

Weeping

It's a retching
of sorrow and sodium.
Sweet saliva sluices
over the brim of
cradled hands.

Water gives its embrace
and unshakable knowledge
that all is not well.

This busted soul widens
letting everything through.
A body's dissent against
umbilicus-deep hauntings.

A cleansing stain
that spreads and seeps
in everyday cycles
of saccharine remorse
and incessant purpose.

Psalm

*Depression is tenacious desert
for gnashing teeth
and braiding rain.*

*You a tomb for my dying;
a womb for my rising.
Your orange-peel curves
reveal acidic plenitude and
threadbare psalms screeching.*

*In your refuge
there is a retching
in which I also rest.
You a prophet
and a Kafka creature
in mid-metamorphosis.*

*The Old Testament says stay.
Stand.
Dwell, darling.*

*To you, Depression,
I protest and prostrate.
Cradle me for perfect asymmetry
to grasp the width and length
and height and depth
of your intimate flesh.*

Aghast

Unarmed on surgeon's table
last cigarette extinguished
eyes seethe with cinder
smolder knowingly with
atlas of lacerations.

Alloyed tools covetous
of skin pristine
bareness beneath
bones snow fragile
tendons and sinew solder.

I am yours recalcitrant
to the revelry of healing
vivisect the malign
this dis-ease denigrates
I want and do not want
regeneration.

The surgeon's hands
skilled as the Talmudist
dissect scintilla of ache
mining beneath grief
to save the lustrous.

Sand suctioned from
teeming throat
barricading breath ways
conduit to life.

Licking my wounds
covered in stitches of cinnamon

tonight in time for Vespers.
Dervish deigning to wail
for something holy to reign
over this post-op body
now made to walk
even though
cast away by my love

Skirting the Wire

Sharing sheets with the woman
not sleeping beside me.
Memories precede the day;
I try to break free
of yesterday's prison.
My fingers form the truth
percolating through my lips:
Self is a verb
for laboring and loving.

Where I ascend
intersects with memory
rotations of sky in my skull.
I am a disciple of poetic baptism
my beginning already begun.
Endless perforations of the membrane
between this life and what is past.

Mind moves to the melodies of ghosts.
Spirit is the transfiguration
of hauntings to holy visitation.
Somatic suffering is my prodigal son,
arms usher in my tenacious survival.

Memory precedes me and is me
it is communal yet deeply personal.
I can no longer detect the boundary
between the living and the resurrected dead.
I am not at war with what passes away
knowing I am a message

to pass from world to world.
Skirting the wire between

memory and chronology:
I am the indescribable intersection,
the aching bridge,
a reluctant instrument
for the reimagining of consciousness.

Slender

Letting you go
is the midwifery of a stillborn
not yet surrendered to soil and pine.
The cruel exposure of what grew concealed
in our womb of pulsing crinoline
gestates in my jaw
giving off a miasma of grief.

Your thumping hips were dense
with perfume and pussy.
You gave my body freedom by fiat.
Your sepulcher still pounds in my gut.

What is salvageable now
can only be resurrected by
a ferocity of the will,
an interruption of the carefully compiled
self-made narrative
that life is this only, will always be
this sorrow.

The modus operandi of grief
is gnomic gasping.
You left your sounds in the walls
and script written on my body.
To reclaim what lives
is to suture where
breath bellows between
threadbare ribs.

There is a speechlessness to the erasure
necessary for healing.

Every morning I must choose
embodiment gentle and rousing,
savoring rinds of routine
and a slender hope for relief.

Touch of Madness

My wild mind
came on last night.
Before it arrived I read
the signs on my palm -
first the conjuring and then
the weight of it all: momentous.

Just a touch of madness comes
with genius. Just a touch, dear
only enough for you to carry.

My holy mad mind
prostrates beneath me
as a weary thread
it's the seam
that keeps my vision
stitched to the tendons of reality.

Loosen your grip on the world
pull on the thread
and watch my soul reveal itself to you
my particularized universe will lay
as a splayed plane
wide enough for you to tour.

Brush my pointed finger with your eye,
follow it down the interstate:
routes and veins
and her hands along the roadside.
Here on the dash

is Mary's delicate eyes like
a flypaper figurine for lesbian love.

I have no right to ask you
but this mind is demanding.
Gather me in the corner where I keep
my fears of being forgotten
clench your hands into a fist
and throw a punch
at the bully, the zealous, the judge.

Let language fill you all the way up
until you feel the alphabet sweep
against your collar.
Edge closer
to my mad process,
my particular genus of spirit.
It is a retching that begins with a sliver
of breath to considering eyes
nicotine to frontal lobe
landing on lips chanting
the name of a mystic.

If I only knew how to offer myself,
to touch madness
and still survive:
primal, free, and bursting.

Movement IV

Rising

"It happens to all of us…God simply keeps reaching down into the dirt of humanity and resurrecting us from the graves we dig for ourselves through our violence, our lies, our selfishness, our arrogance, and our addiction. And God keeps loving us back to life over and over."
    – Nadia Bolz-Weber

A Piece of Work

I think of her inside the grammar
of my grief, my wanting rests
in the palms of swollen vowels;
wanting carries its shame
inside the unsayable stuff of night.

What can be said
beats at the backs of teeth
dissolving the miasma of silence.
Preening in the ovate omega,
I offer my dying
to soft necks
and curvatures of collars:
the sacramental language of bodies
who accompany me through the breaking.
Wounds become windows
so that I'm both blood and beauty.

Written on my body
are her sounds
and a gnomic gospel
preventing the erasure of my divinity,
building bridges of bone
compiling verses for a piece of work.

I am God's piece of work, meant
to limn the names of things felt
for which the jaw has no shape;
to undress my wounds,
barefaced but unembarrassed.
This word work is a rending
of syllabic wrists.

In the Land of the Living

All of my life
was lived last week
like prayer beads
strung on trees
every mystery of the rosary
hung root to blossom
on the street corner where everyone speeds.

Everyone we know
in every metaphysic place
liminal phases
we've all walked
in collective solitude
isolated exuberant sorrow.
We are daily nearing ourselves,
reaching for connection.

Walking this street
lit by tungsten filament
and mendicant stars
begging for beatification
or just a taste of creation
to suffer as the prophets
to dance as the saints.

In the land of the living
where we are all lost
where we solve problems
    but never get ahead
where my girl wraps me safe in her arms

where we can't find satisfying work.

Here in the land of the living
we do good and we do harm
everyone has an answer

                    and no answers at all

we lose ourselves
until we walk against the wind
and know we each have a soul
to break adumbrate expiate
the blessed transgressions
of being alive.

Therapy

Twenty times over
as if breathing
my jaw descends
discarding poetry
to call a knife a knife.

My tongue splits over a crinoline
for you to lance with boned
fingers elbow deep in the hiddenness
of this wound.

Oxygen plumes
here: a lung between armchairs
inhaling alarm clocks
minutes counted in the dance
of crossing and uncrossing legs.

I take you for Jung's dream
or Linehan's gospel.
Can you see the accidental saints
we've become.
You already know
what breaks in us
where to look;
even the volume of an eyelash
can cast a shadow.

With the neurosis
of a dancer en face
I see defeat

you see only the rehearsal;

these rituals of mercy
yield honey, holy water,
and brutal baptism.

Near the closing
you sing the throat-hum
of a practiced hymn:
stay here.
stay.
here.

Open Mic

Here we pour our bodies like wine
for the queerest of communions
spilling hungry as the live animal
beating at the backs of our teeth.

Today I found the husk of a skin
discarded because of a revelation
received at the mic;
we hounded at the sight
of their lavishly dark discovery.

We are being born gorgeous
at this banquet of opening eyes.
Running waters satisfy the thirst
of our obsidian gods.

At the mic,
we love magnanimously
and roar with the sounds
of belonging.

Resurrection

You have to die a thousand deaths
to rest on a bay leaf
and run your fingers down
a river of honey.

Watch beside yourself
with a brazen ache
a flesh wound releasing
milk and Sunday hymns.
Dying a small death tastes
like an altar pulled straight
out of Gethsemane.

The real world doesn't care
whether you drool cathedrals
in your sleep anymore
or where you've hid the dove
you usually keep in your ear.

Find some peace in planting
relics below piles of laundry,
sweeping every dirty bit beneath
the floorboards scentless as gold,
new as today's skin.

Whatever this life means
I know we must do this
one thousand times over.

Poet Priest

All I wish
is to stand before God
at the end of my life and say,
I was your poet, I was your priest.

Unbind(ing)

"Writing is my passion. Words are the way to know ecstasy. Without them life is barren. The poet insists, language is a body of suffering and when you take up language you take up the suffering too. All my life I have been suffering for words. Words have been the source of pain and the way to heal."

- bell hooks

This is an ending that is not an ending. In the telling of my story, in fragments as they live in my mind, I am unbound.

The wounds that for so long have been bound by all the ways

I have been silent and afraid.

In writing there is risk. The risk of being known. Visible.

This is my terror. My freedom.

Brokenness is the heart of a spiritual life. Self-help books advertise the possibility of attaining wholeness, of healing. Complete. For once and all. I cannot get behind this ideology. Healing is vastly more complex than these sources offer. We are all, of course, limited in our expression. Language is limiting. Words can get at, very close, to meaning *but never quite arrives.*

It's been my experience that the "once and for all" mentality is bullshit. No real change or transformation happens with one powerful night or the moment upon hearing a profound teaching. It is a process that never ends.

This is the reason for the parentheses in the title of this book. I am unbound in the expression but unbinding in my lived experience. My identity as a teacher, minister, poet, lesbian is the source of my woundedness, because I occupy peripheral spaces, but my marginalization is also the basis of my power. Being marginalized does not mean the absence of power, it is the presence of voice, the strength of empathy. My wounds are a sanguine pulse of how I love and why I am loved.

All the times I have strived to be entirely professional, withdrawing my emotions, self-policing my identity, leaving the unwelcomed parts of me outside the central places of power I die many deaths. The rhetoric around adulthood and the workplace frustrate me. I want to be all of who I am in every space. Yet the reality is that every community will disappoint at one time; they will say something offensive; they will act in inconsiderate ways; or I will transgress and be the source of something offensive. Always the navigating of how to speak and interact with each other.

Vulnerability must be vigilant because we are disappointing beings. We hurt each other. We cause harm. We expose, leaving another unsafe. We don't know each other's experience.

We ask and listen. And try our best. But we will disappoint.

I still believe that vulnerability is a necessity to live authentically and allow others to be authentic.

Here is the rub: we cannot expect authenticity if we are not willing to be authentic. Honesty is terrifying. But it's the only way to live fully human. In my short lifetime of going through the motions of accomplishing things, earning degrees, progressing in my career the most meaningful moments have been the intimate knowing of another person. I have come to believe that that is all that matters. Really. My vulnerability has been taken advantage of, it has been called names, it has put my job at risk. But nothing is worth it unless I am myself.

So, I unbind. I loosen the bandages one at a time and allow myself to be visible. To be seen is the most remarkable feeling. For someone to get me, to open their eyes wide and limn every part of me, is to treat me as human and holy.

To commit myself to do the same for someone else is a conversion to the holy. Every time.

I AM WHO I AM.

I live in this skin holding the identities I claim right now, and I am always seeking myself. My life is the seeking of myself. In this seeking, I am wounded. Wounded by my own transgressions that take me away from my truest self and the transgressions of others as they are distanced from themselves.

These wounds are five in number; they are dozens; they are never ending and always deepening.

I daily watch as red divets in my skin adorn themselves with raiment, the thinnest veils of shimmering pink new skin. Filling in the lack, the empty space. But they remain. Some still sting, and others are reminders of what I've been through; I try to look at them without judgement, gentle.

There is resurrection in healing. Resurrection happens when I unbind a wound and allow another to see my pain, knowing they are not alone in their pain. I rise to God when I rise to another;

when I can say, Look I have hurt in this way. It leaves a mark and never goes away completely. But now

I can connect with you.

This is how I feel. This is what I know.

Here are my wounds.

I hope they are useful to you.

Acknowledgements

I owe a great deal of thanks to those who have supported my writing. One year ago, I walked heavy with grief into the Queer and Trans Open Mic. I had found my family. These poems would not exist without all of you.

Thank you to my parents and sister, Michaela, for giving me space to find my own path, knowing that I don't like being 'telled' what to do.

Thank you to my friends for their love & encouragement. For Erin, Estee, Molleen, and Nichole. Thank you to Darleen for your wise guidance over the past seven years.

Thank you to Liz for staying with me, even now we are together. Much gratitude to Shaunna for keeping it weird, and always lovely; and love for all of my teachers at Shawl-Anderson Dance Center for sustaining me in heart and body.

Thank you to the brilliant Kin Folkz, my friend and mentor, for never letting me forget on whose shoulders I stand.

Immense gratitude to Taylor Duckett and Conviction 2 Change Publishing (Conviction 2 Change LLC). It's been a pleasure to collaborate with you on this project.

All the snaps for my community at the Oakland LGBTQ Center.

About the Author

Asher Marron is an Oakland poet and educator. She holds a Master of Theology from the Franciscan School of Theology and a Bachelor of Arts in history from Mills College. She is currently an MFA student at San Francisco State University. Asher's poetry aims to beatify queer bodies by expressing the complexity of queer identity through spiritual aesthetics.

Connect with Asher Marron:

Facebook: Asher Marron

Instagram: @ashermarron

Website: www.ashermarron.com